S T O R M

D E V O T I O N S

STORM DEVOTIONS

GOD'S WORD TO GET YOU THROUGH

DAVID
WASHINGTON JR.

Pleasant Word (a division of WinePress Publishing, PO Box 428, Enumclaw, WA 98022) functions only as book publisher. As such, the ultimate design, content, editorial accuracy, and views expressed or implied in this work are those of the author.

Unless otherwise noted, all Scriptures are taken from the *New American Standard Bible*, Copyright © 1960, 1962, 1963, 1968, 1971, 1972, 1973, 1975, 1977, 1995 by The Lockman Foundation. Used by permission.

Scripture references marked KJV are taken from the *King James Version* of the Bible.

ISBN 13: 978-1-4141-1440-8
ISBN 10: 1-4141-1440-0
Library of Congress Catalog Card Number: 2009903169

CONTENTS

INTRODUCTION

Be grateful and give thanks. God's goodness and mercy have been following you all the days of your life! Even when we are in the midst storms, trials, and challenges, God is still in control. Be encouraged because though you may not see it, you can be sure that God's hand is on your life and if your life is in His hands, you will not be snatched by the enemy. Try Him and most certainly, He will pour out a blessing.

Instructions on how to use this devotional

I praise God that you have chosen to read this devotional. God placed it on my heart to write and share this devotional with you so that you might have a weekly tool to study, reflect and apply God's word. When you encounter life storms you will find these godly and practical principles will help guide you through your storms. There are fifty-two chapters that correspond to the fifty-two weeks in a given calendar year. You will read a chapter at the beginning of your week and think through and plan out how to apply that principle throughout your week. May you be richly blessed and may God transform your life in a most magnificent way.

CHAPTER 1

IT'S A NEW SEASON

We all know New Year's resolutions do not work. We make them and are disciplined about keeping them for about three weeks. While a resolution may not be what we need as we start a new year, we do need to be transformed (changed into Christ's image).

The Bible says we can all become new creatures when we accept Christ: "Therefore from now on we recognize no one according to the flesh; even though we have known Christ according to the flesh, yet now we know Him in this way no longer. Therefore if anyone is in Christ, he is a new creature; the old things passed away; behold, new things have come" (2 Cor. 5:16-17). This scripture implies that a true commitment to Christ should result in changes of our heart, mind, and spirit. Once we make this commitment to Christ, we should strive to be Christ's ambassadors.

The best change you can make is to become all Christ has called you to be. Three things will bring this change:

1. Acknowledge that Christ is the only source for a changed life;
2. Confess and repent from the sin that is keeping you in your old creature;
3. Surrender and believe God will change you from the inside out.

ASK YOURSELF

What do I need to do to be an ambassador for Christ?

PONDER THIS

When you received Christ, you became a new creature.

CHAPTER 2

GET OUT OF THE GATES

Satan hates new beginnings and fresh starts. That's why Scripture teaches us that God wants us to feel continuously fresh and renewed. In Romans 12:1-3, Paul writes that we must be transformed by the renewing of our minds so we can prove God's acceptable and perfect will. In Psalms, we are reminded to sing unto the Lord a new song and a new praise. "He put a new song in my mouth, a song of praise to our God; Many will see and fear And will trust in the LORD" (Ps. 40:3). God wants to guide each one of us into a constant and fresh renewal of our heart, attitude, and perspective toward life and His will for it.

In His divine wisdom, God knew we would be bombarded with constant challenges and trials on this side of heaven. Satan works hard to keep us from getting refreshed and renewed! Yet God's Word teaches us that we must not yield to Satan's schemes.

In horse racing, the term "get out of the gates" means that a great start is vital to an outstanding finish. Without a great start, a successful finish is more difficult to achieve.

In the same way, as we start this new season it's important to "get out of the gates" with a fresh attitude, a heart of thanksgiving, and a new sense of praise and joy! Forgetting those things that are behind, press on toward the mark of the high calling of Christ Jesus. (Phil. 3:14).

ASK YOURSELF

What is my strategy this year to "get out of the gates"?

PONDER THIS

This season, this day, and this moment of revelation are awesome times because you still have breath in your body and the ability to get out of the gate and to start fresh.

CHAPTER 3

PREPARATION

Whether you hold a title or not in the church, you are called to be a leader for God's kingdom. The calling to lead, to serve God, or to minister to others, is a calling of preparation. After all, no soldier goes to war without getting basic training first. Anyone who is fit to work for the kingdom of God, must first recognize the enormity of God's call to serve Him. This will bring you to a greater sense of humility as you recognize the awesomeness of the God who created you and who has granted you the privilege of being His servant. A servant who is called, must be willing to yield to God's authority over his or her life. What soldier becomes a great leader without first being a great follower?

Are you prepared to become a great kingdom servant? Ask yourself these questions:

- Do I have a hunger and a thirst for a relationship with Christ? (If it's easy for you to go for extended periods without wanting to talk to Christ, you're not prepared).
- Do I have a hunger and thirst for God's agenda? (If a burden for lost souls isn't part of your DNA, you're not prepared. Great servants want to please God. Everything else is secondary).
- Do I have less hunger for carnality and sin? Sin will make you sick if the Holy Spirit is active and dominant in your life. (If habitual sins—little white lies, integrity issues, pride, a rebellious spirit—are a major part of your life, you're not prepared).

- Do I have a hunger and thirst for the richness of God's Word? Great servants love God's Word. They study it, read it, meditate on it, and attempt to live it. (If you don't study to show yourself approved, you're not prepared).
- Do I have a kingdom mindset? Where does what you do connect to the kingdom? (If your life is still compartmentalized into "my church life" and "my other life," you're not prepared).

ASK YOURSELF

Have you been seeking a position or preparing for the position God has for you?

PONDER THIS

God already knows what He has in store for your ministry, but He is waiting to see how faithful you are.

CHAPTER 4

GETTING THROUGH WEARINESS

Ministry is hard work. Serving Christ and serving others is a never-ending process. Those of us who are serving Christ faithfully often find ourselves getting weary. Why do we get weary? Sometimes we are overstretched because we are doing more than we are called to do. Other times we are working outside of our spiritual gifts.

Most often, we get tired because we have forgotten to abide in the Master. John 15:5 says, "I am the vine, you are the branches; he who abides in Me and I in him, he bears much fruit, for apart from Me you can do nothing." In other words, we are to rely on Him for strength. We are not supposed to try to find it on our own. The Lord expects us to work closely with Him while we use the gifts He provides.

How do we move away from God? When we fail to do our daily devotions—praying and meditating on God's Word—we fail to nurture (abide) our relationship with Christ. Initially we do not realize it, but over time, we become spiritually weak and tired. As a result, we find ourselves trying to produce fruit instead of bearing it. However, as the scripture says, we cannot produce fruit. We only can bear it by remaining near to Christ.

ASK YOURSELF

How can I improve my walk in ministry by remaining with Christ?

PONDER THIS

Ministry is not about doing. It's about becoming!

CHAPTER 5

A GIFT WE MUST SHARE

Thank God, that Jesus' precious blood paid for the gift of eternal life! This is a gift we cannot earn—even through good works. We must accept the gift of eternal life wholly and freely. Then we must be discipled and transformed into Christ's image. This is God's plan for us.

I pastor a church that's main purpose is to reach out to those who don't have this gift of eternal life. This is why we envision ourselves as a "lighthouse of disciples." Our vision is to be a place where families will grow in the Lord and the community will be spiritually revived. We want to raise up Christian soldiers who will spread the gospel throughout the world.

Hopefully, you are part of a fellowship with these same goals. We all know of churches that have lost sight of Jesus' Great Commission (See Matt. 28:18-20). This is sad because what good is a lighthouse if it never produces light? It is up to each one of us to take the torch of light where there is darkness. The Word says that God wishes no one would perish (See Matt. 18:14). Therefore, it is our responsibility as Christians to have the same desire and heart as Christ. That means we need to share the gospel.

Reach someone for Christ this week. Ask God to direct you to an un-churched person—then, nurture that relationship. Invite that person to church with you. Pray that he or she might receive the free gift of eternal life as you have.

ASK YOURSELF

How can I be a lighthouse and reach out to those who do not have the gift of eternal life?

PONDER THIS

Christians care about the things that Jesus cares about.

CHAPTER 6

CROSS THAT BRIDGE AND ENTER THE VISION

It is often difficult to see where God is leading us, so taking a step toward that vision normally requires us to make an adjustment by faith. When this happens, Satan gets us to function in self-doubt and fear. As a result, many people are still on the other side of the bridge with only a blurred memory of that vision God gave them for their lives. Many have been on the other side of the bridge for so long that the vision has almost disappeared due to sin and disobedience. They find themselves living lives they weren't meant to live.

It's never too late for a person to choose the path God has ordained for his or her life. Sure, you may have delayed your season and missed out on some blessings, but God promised He would not leave us nor forsake us. In Jeremiah 29:11, the prophet Jeremiah wrote the words of the Lord: "'For I know the plans that I have for you,' declares the LORD, 'plans for welfare and not for calamity to give you a future and a hope.'" The same principle that applied to Israel during their Babylonian captivity applies to us today.

That vision God gave you for your life can still come to fruition. Cross that bridge. Begin to walk the path God has for your life!

ASK YOURSELF

Am I living out God's vision for my life?

PONDER THIS

There is still time for you to change paths.

CHAPTER 7

FAILURE IS NOT FINAL

So much of what we learn in life comes as a result of trial and error. Failure is a necessary part of the equation whether we are learning to walk, learning how to ride a bike, or learning how to live out God's Word. Satan wants us to believe that our failures and mistakes are the end of the story for us as believers.

Every great biblical leader endured some kind of failure. In fact, many of the great leaders failed more than once. Moses committed a murder before God called him to lead the Israelites from slavery in Egypt. Abraham lied, refused to trust God, and conceived Ishmael with his wife's maid, after which God formed him into a man of great faith. King David committed adultery and murder in the midst of becoming Israel's greatest king. Even the apostle Peter denied Christ in a most critical moment before becoming the leader of the New Testament church.

As these men show us, our failures are not final. Instead, failures are the building blocks for future victories! The apostle Paul wrote in Philippians 3:13-14, "Brethren, I do not regard myself as having laid hold of it yet; but one thing I do: *forgetting what lies behind* and reaching forward to what lies ahead, I press on toward the goal for the prize of the upward call of God in Christ Jesus" (emphasis added).

When you experience your next failure, error, or mistake, learn from it, then shake it off, forget about it, and press on.

Ask Yourself

How do I handle failure?

Ponder This

God uses our failures to further His work in us.

CHAPTER 8

THE RAT RACE ISN'T YOUR RACE

We live in a culture that embraces stress. Busyness and constantly being on the run have become the norms in our society. However, as we examine Scripture, we find that God never intended this for His people. God clearly says in His Word that we must take time regularly to worship Him and to rest our bodies (See Ex. 16:22-23).

Too much stress can lead to heart disease, high blood pressure, headaches, and many other disorders. Satan uses stress and the poor management of it to wreak havoc in Christians' lives. We must recognize his tactics and confront them by not yielding to them.

Are you running like a chicken with its head cut off? Why? Is running doing you any good? Are you living in constant stress? Is God getting the glory through your life or are you too busy to give God what belongs to Him?

Remember, you have been fearfully and wonderfully made for God's glory. Slow down! Get out of the rat race. You're not a rat, so that race was not meant for you.

ASK YOURSELF

How can I reduce the stress in my life?

PONDER THIS

God wants you to rest in Him.

CHAPTER 9

GOD'S PROVISION NEVER FAILS

In John 21, the recently resurrected Jesus appears to His disciples on the seashore. Early in the chapter, Simon Peter, Thomas, and Nathanael go fishing all night only to come up empty. Just as dawn is breaking through, Jesus emerges and instructs them to cast their nets again on the right-hand side of the boat. Interestingly enough, these disciples were professional fishermen and had plenty of expertise in the field of fishing. Even though Christ was instructing them about something they already knew, they immediately obeyed Him. They caught so many fish that their nets were completely full!

What can we learn from this? The first point is that God's instructions do not always have to make sense to us. I'm sure the disciples must have thought for a brief moment, *Why is Jesus trying to tell us how to do our jobs? We've already been here fishing all night long and have caught nothing.* In the same way, we as Christians often try, either consciously or subconsciously, to ignore God's instructions because we think we are experts on the matter at hand. However, as Jesus showed His fishing disciples, God's exercises are never fruitless. He does everything with a purpose.

Another point I love about this story is that God never miscalculates His provision. When we move on our own accord, instead of waiting on God, we always miss a step or two. We often try to do things our way only to discover that our basket isn't big enough and our shoulders aren't broad enough. Yet if we place ourselves in His will, we find we can do everything He asks of us, including catching just the right amount of fish.

ASK YOURSELF

Am I following God's instructions even when they do not make sense to me?

PONDER THIS

When we as Christians move in obedience to God, His plans always work.

CHAPTER 10

OWNING THE VISION

Proverbs 29:18 (KJV) says, "Where there is no vision, the people perish." The church that I pastor recognizes God's vision. God has done wonderful things because of it. It has come with trials, challenges, and lessons in perseverance and faith. I warned my church that we would struggle physically, financially, emotionally, and spiritually. We continue to do so. Yet we also experience great seasons of learning to walk by faith and not by sight.

I truly believe that God loves us so much that He allows us to experience these struggles to teach us how to be more faithful and dependent on Him. God, in His divine wisdom, asks all of us at one time or another, "Where will you now turn in your season of famine?" If we're honest with ourselves, we only can draw one conclusion. That is, God is the only one we can turn to. James explains the rewards when we do:

> Consider it all joy, my brethren, when you encounter various trials, knowing that the testing of your faith produces endurance. And let endurance have its perfect result, so that you may be perfect and complete, lacking in nothing.
>
> —James 1:2-4

Take ownership of the vision God has given you. Do your part and take responsibility for becoming who God designed you to be!

Ask Yourself

How can I embrace my faith lessons and trust God to be a good steward over that with which He has entrusted me?

Ponder This

God is not interested in leaving His people hanging, for that would be a poor testimony unto Himself.

CHAPTER 11

STUCK ON GO?

Remember playing board games as a child and getting frustrated because you could not get off the starting space? Didn't it always seem like all the other players were making progress toward the finish line, but you could not launch from "Go"?

What an illustration this is for those who are stuck in their walks with Jesus! Unlike a board game, where the ability to move forward is based on rolling dice or drawing a card, Christians get spiritually stuck due to their own lack of obedience. That's why God's Word challenges us to "walk by the Spirit, [so] you will not carry out the desire of the flesh" (Gal. 5:16).

"Desires of the flesh" are those things that are against God. The Bible lists them as sexual immorality and impurity, gossip, jealousy, outbursts of anger, strife, causing dissension and disputes, etc. If any of these traits are consistently in your life and have been for some time, you are stuck on "Go."

Today would be a good day to repent and renew your commitment to walking in the Spirit of God. Walking in the Spirit means walking in a manner consistently pleasing to God. When you walk in the Spirit, you exhibit the fruit of the Spirit mentioned in Galatians 5:22-23—love, joy, peace, patience, kindness, goodness, faithfulness, gentleness, and self-control.

ASK YOURSELF

How can I move forward in my Christian walk?

PONDER THIS

Walking in the Spirit means obeying all that God's Word commands us to do—not only what we want to do.

CHAPTER 12

GET REAL TO GET CHANGED!

My church is not a place for people who just want to be religious—meaning those who want to attend a Sunday morning service but have no real desire to have their lives transformed by and to be conformed to Christ's image. Religious people are those who attend church all their lives but bear no fruit. They are still mean, malicious, gossiping, messy, selfish, self-centered, and faithless. What they appear to be on Sunday morning may not be the same as what they are Monday through Saturday.

Scripture teaches us that when people really commit their lives to Christ, they become new creatures:

> Therefore if anyone is in Christ, he is a new creature; the old things passed away; behold, new things have come.
> —2 Cor. 5:17

The word *creature* in the original Greek language is *ktisis*, which means "original creation." So the teaching here is that when we are surrendered fully to God through a relationship with Christ, we can become all God wants us to be. The moment we fully and sincerely surrender, God begins to mold, shape, and transform us into what He designed us to be.

To walk as God has called us to walk, we have to "get real." We must move from the mindset of *looking* like a Christian to *being* a Christian. We need to make a conscious decision to be changed by acknowledging our need for Christ and turning from a life of sin. We also must pray and ask God to work supernaturally in our lives through the power of His Holy Spirit.

ASK YOURSELF

How can I get real and get changed?

PONDER THIS

We must make a daily decision to pick up our cross and walk with Him.

CHAPTER 13

THE MEANING OF LIFE

How precious life is! The world, especially America, has adopted a "seize the day" mentality, which calls for everyone to eat, drink, and be merry. However, those who live and think this way do not know the meaning of life, nor do they understand the purpose of their existence. Living for the day as if it was one big party implies that today is all there is, and that living in and for the moment is beneficial. Too often, it takes a near-death experience to get people to consider what life really means and how much we should value it. We sometimes take for granted the continued grace and mercy our Almighty God extends to us.

Jesus tells us in John 14:6, "I am the way, and the truth, and the life; no one comes to the Father but through Me." In this text, Jesus gives us a solemn statement about the meaning and purpose of life. He tells us He is life. Therefore, life has no meaning, no substance, and no real value apart from Him.

Jesus is so serious about this that He implores us, His creation, to submit, surrender, and receive Him. In receiving Him, we receive life. We come to the revelation of life's true meaning. In receiving Christ as our Redeemer, Lord, and Savior, we gain new meaning, new purpose, new guidance, and full truth.

ASK YOURSELF

How can I fully grasp Christ, now, while I've got lots of life in front of me?

PONDER THIS

Anything less than receiving Christ and walking with Him is meaningless.

CHAPTER 14

WALK IN INTEGRITY

A phrase that is often used to describe integrity is, "A man is only as good as his word." A person's truth and honesty are best measured by evaluating how closely aligned his actions are with the words he speaks.

God knows and cares how we live. Luke 12:1-3 reads, "Beware of the leaven of the Pharisees, which is hypocrisy. But there is nothing covered up that will not be revealed, and hidden that will not be known. Accordingly, whatever you have said in the dark will be heard in the light, and what you have whispered in the inner rooms will be proclaimed upon the housetops."

Those who are in the church must learn to walk with the utmost integrity. We need to be willing to live out God's uncompromised Word without apology. The body of Christ no longer can afford to preach one Word on Sunday and live out another Word the rest of the week. When we live without integrity, we ruin our witness to a lost world. We don't give God an opportunity to work in and through us. God can and will work only through those whom He can trust.

ASK YOURSELF

Can God trust me to work in me?

PONDER THIS

God knows everything you think, say, and do.

CHAPTER 15

THE CHURCH CAN'T LIVE
WITHOUT IT

The church lives as its members give, so it is the duty of each Christian to share in the financial responsibilities of his or her church on a regular basis. My church does not assess the amount of tithes or offerings each member should give. We feel that each member and/or family should decide this. We encourage them to pray about their finances and the amount they will give.

By the way, the idea of tithing wasn't invented by greedy pastors. God ordained it. Read this passage from 2 Corinthians 9:6-8, paying special attention to verse seven:

> Now this I say, he who sows sparingly shall also reap sparingly, and he who sows bountifully shall also reap bountifully. Each one must do just as he has purposed in his heart, not grudgingly or under compulsion, for God loves a cheerful giver. And God is able to make all grace abound to you, so that always having all sufficiency in everything, you may have an abundance for every good deed.

God commands us to be faithful in our tithing. Your church needs your faithful tithing and giving to live, prosper, and to do the Lord's work. God delights in His children's generous giving. He also promises to extend grace and provision as we faithfully give to the work of His kingdom agenda.

The Lord has given believers a divine assignment to build His kingdom. Let us embrace this privilege with our faithful service and giving.

ASK YOURSELF

What does the Lord deserve from me so His name will be glorified and His work fulfilled?

PONDER THIS

God loves a cheerful giver.

CHAPTER 16

EXCELLENCE IS GOD'S STANDARD

Have you ever walked into someone's house and noticed it was extremely untidy or even dirty? If you're like me, you probably surmised that the entire house was untidy or dirty, and that the people living there were always untidy and dirty. Granted, this might be an unfair judgment. Perhaps the homeowner was just having an off day. But in most cases, we believe what we see.

While image is not everything, having a sincere godly character is. The great philosopher Aristotle said, "We are what we repeatedly do. Excellence, then, is not an act, but a habit." This quote is profound because it speaks of discipline and excellence in terms of character and personality.

God's Word also speaks of excellence. In 2 Peter 1:3, Peter wrote, "Seeing that His divine power has granted to us everything pertaining to life and godliness, through the true knowledge of Him who called us by His own glory and excellence."

Excellence is God's standard for everything. As His representatives, we too must walk in excellence. Whatever we do in our lives, whether it is managing our ministries, our jobs, our marriages, or our families, we must do it with excellence. God is glorified when His standards of excellence are demonstrated through our lives.

ASK YOURSELF

How can I clean my "house" to make it worthy of God's excellence?

PONDER THIS

If we profess to be God's children we must walk and live in excellence.

CHAPTER 17

FAITH AND OBEDIENCE GO HAND IN HAND

John McArthur writes in his book, *Truth for Today*, "It's not faith plus obedience that equals salvation, but obedient faith that equals salvation. True faith is verified in your obedience to God. Because Jesus is Lord, He demands obedience."

What a powerful statement that is! We live in a world where too many people claim to be Christians because they have faith in Jesus Christ. Many of the people who make this claim do not understand that their faith in Christ demands obedience. Jesus said, "He who has My commandments and keeps them is the one who loves Me" (John 14:21).

Scripture teaches us that the Holy Spirit draws us to God by our faith. Faith then triggers our obedience to Christ and His commands. As we develop and grow as Christians, it is our intimate love relationship with Him that moves us to obey Him. Spending time with Christ in His Word, through prayer and devotion, causes our confident assurance (faith) in Christ to grow. We then learn that obedience is a must and not an option. In other words, as you mature as a disciple, you obey Christ not because it is your duty or your pastor told you to do it. You obey Him because you love Him too much not to!

If you have received and loved Christ by faith, obedience will follow. If you have a problem with obedience, then you also will have a problem loving Christ. To know Him is to love Him. To love Him is to obey Him.

ASK YOURSELF

How am I being disobedient to the Lord?

PONDER THIS

Obedience shows evidence of faith.

CHAPTER 18

IS TITHING FOR THE
NEW TESTAMENT CHRISTIAN?

To give 10 percent or not to give, that is the question. Or is it?

Actually, giving 10 percent is neither the question nor the issue when it comes to stewardship and tithing. A Bible scholar could argue that Christians are no longer under the law. Therefore, the tithe (10 percent) is not required. However, anyone who attempts to make that argument does not fully understand God's love and grace.

It is true that God does not require Christians to give 10 percent of their income to Him. However, Scripture clearly teaches that Christ did not abolish the law, but fulfilled it in the sense that He perfected it. Because of His redemptive work, the requirements, calling, privilege, obedience, and benefits of being in relationship with Him are greater than they were with the Old Covenant.

The New Covenant in Christ calls us to give everything. This includes our lives, hearts, time, talents, bodies, and, yes, our treasure for the cause of the gospel. How can we figure out what to give to God? Second Corinthians 9:7 says that we ought to give as we purpose in our hearts, not grudgingly or under compulsion, because God loves a cheerful giver.

Translated, that means:

1. You give to Him, not to a local church or pastor.
2. Your giving should reflect your love-relationship with Him. (Wow, thinking of it that way doesn't make 10 percent difficult at all!)
3. You should give generously to God for His kingdom work and for the agenda of the gospel.

A person who has faith in Jesus Christ does not worry about whether or not the New Testament commands tithing, but about how to be more like our generous Christ. However, giving does not earn that relationship. It is a result of it. We are granted grace through faith, not through tithing.

ASK YOURSELF

How should I adjust my giving to demonstrate my faithfulness in carrying out God's kingdom agenda?

PONDER THIS

Tithing is a privilege that results from Christ's redemptive work in us.

CHAPTER 19

RELIGION VS. RELATIONSHIP

I am convinced that there are too many people sitting on church pews every Sunday who only experience "religion" and not an authentic relationship with Jesus Christ. The evidence of this is in the fruit that comes from their lives. Jesus said in Matthew 7 that we can know "true" Christians by their fruit—what they do in His name.

People who proclaim to be Christians but never bear fruit through their attitudes, conduct, speech, relationships, service to God, giving, loving, etc., are living a lie. True Christians not only bear fruit, but they are convicted to change the error of their sinful ways. Any Christian who continues in sin without conviction does not have a healthy relationship with Jesus Christ. Jesus and His Word always lead to transformation.

Jesus makes a more powerful statement in Matthew 7:21-23 when he says, "Not everyone who says to Me, 'Lord, Lord,' will enter the kingdom of heaven, but he who does the will of My Father who is in heaven will enter. Many will say to Me on that day, 'Lord, Lord, did we not prophesy in Your name, and in Your name cast out demons, and in Your name perform many miracles?' And then I will declare to them, 'I never knew you; *depart from me, you who practice lawlessness*'" (emphasis added).

The bottom line here is that Jesus declares that those who attend church, sing in the choir, preach the gospel, serve on auxiliaries, and so on, are not necessarily in relationship with Him. In the end judgment, this fact will be revealed.

Do you fake it to make it? Get in a real relationship with the Lord today by completely surrendering your life to Him!

ASK YOURSELF

What fruit am I bearing for Christ? What sins do I need to surrender to Him?

PONDER THIS

No matter how much good you do, God holds you accountable for the sin in your life.

CHAPTER 20

YOUR ATTITUDE DETERMINES YOUR ALTITUDE

Doctors and scientists have documented that a terminally ill patient who has a will to fight and to live typically lives longer than a patient who does not have that same attitude. Life is really about how we decide to approach it!

The Bible says it this way in Proverbs 23:7, "As he thinks within himself, so he is." What a profound and indicting statement! In essence, how each person thinks about himself, and how he lives out that perception through his actions, are major factors in determining his destiny.

This teaching is not saying we can speak things into existence or we can manipulate world events with mind power. What God is saying in His Word is that the promises He has laid out for us can be fulfilled in our lives as we choose to believe them by faith. Faith then must move from our heads and hearts to our actions.

Therefore, if you live what you believe, your actions will reflect that attitude. For example, if you believe God has a plan for your life, then by faith you must live every day with a passion and purpose, expecting God to use you and execute His plan through you. Does your attitude say, "Yes, Lord, I believe in what You promise, and my attitude and actions demonstrate that?" How far you go in your life journey with God, starts with having the right attitude!

ASK YOURSELF

What do I think about the following:

- My life
- What God thinks about me

PONDER THIS

Live every day in such a way that your attitude reflects where
you're headed—heaven!

CHAPTER 21

THE HOLY SPIRIT IS GOD, NOT A SPIRITUAL GIFT

There is a lot of misunderstanding and incorrect teaching in the body of Christ regarding the ministry and person of the Holy Spirit. Some denominations even teach that the Holy Spirit is a spiritual gift from God, evidenced by speaking in a heavenly language.

Scripture does not affirm this teaching. The Holy Spirit, also known as the Holy Ghost, is a person. He is part of the Trinity or triune God. In John 16, Jesus tells us exactly who the Holy Spirit is. He also tells His disciples in John 14 and 16 that He is going to ascend back into heaven. He says that He will send the Holy Spirit, the Helper, to those who believe in Him.

Jesus says in John that the Holy Sprit has several functions:

- Helper (14:16)
- Teacher (14:26)
- Reminder (14:26)
  The One who convicts us of sins (16:8-9)
- The One who empowers us to live righteously (16:10)
- Guide into all truth (16:13)
- Discerner (16:13)
- Glorifier of Christ
- Witness for Him (16:14)

The Holy Spirit has a distinct role to play because He is God who dwells within true believers. Ephesians 1:13 says that at the moment a Christian believes and trusts in Christ, he or she is sealed with the Holy Spirit. The Spirit desires to fill us and to direct the course of our lives, thoughts, and actions. The Holy Spirit cannot be caught like a cold. He is a person who helps us in the Christian journey!

ASK YOURSELF

How does the Holy Spirit work in my life?

PONDER THIS

The Holy Spirit is not something we can attain. He is part of God's grace when we receive Christ.

CHAPTER 22

BE FILLED WITH THE SPIRIT

Ephesians 5:18 tells us, "Do not get drunk with wine, for that is dissipation, but be filled with the Spirit." The command to "be filled with the Spirit" is written in the present tense imperative, which means it is a daily requirement. In other words, we are to be filled constantly and every day of our lives.

How do you know when someone is filled with God's Spirit? A person who is filled with God's Spirit is consistent in his or her Christ-like character and actions. Christ's personal manifestation is demonstrated continuously in the life of someone who is filled with the Spirit. This is evident both in the person's obedience to Scripture and to God's commands. Additionally, Spirit-filled Christians are consistent in their conduct, speech, and daily actions. Christ is like a sweet fragrance that permeates their beings.

How can believers ensure they are constantly being filled with God's Spirit? Believers must die to self daily. They must replace self-centeredness with Christ centeredness. When we are self-centered, our sinful nature has more control than God's Spirit has within us. When we die to self, Christ becomes prominent, preeminent, and permanent.

Believers must pray daily for God to fill them with the Holy Spirit. Remember, talk is cheap. A believer must pray with the earnest desire for the prayer to come to fruition. God honors a sincere prayer that lines up with His Word.

Ask Yourself

Can people tell if I am filled with the Holy Spirit? Why or why not?

PONDER THIS

Ask God to fill you with the Holy Spirit by praying, "Lord, fill me with Your Holy Spirit. Have Your way with me, Lord. Control my mind and my body. Let me glorify You in all that I do!"

CHAPTER 23

WHY DO YOU PRAISE?

I've been in churches that were completely dry. By that, I mean that there was no emotion, poor music, no spirit, and no praise. I've also been in churches where there was a lot of ranting, shouting, dancing, and praising. However, in reality, that too was dry because the experience had no purpose or sincerity. It was strictly emotional.

Praise and worship must be rooted in a sincere understanding of, and relationship with, God. We praise God because we value Him. We worship God because we honor Him according to His Word. When a person praises and worships with sincerity, that person comes into God's presence. Both the praiser and God feel the joy of praise (See Ps. 16:11).

Praise comes from a Latin word meaning "value" or "price." Thus, to give God praise is to proclaim His merit or worth. When people praise, they are responding to the way God has revealed Himself to them. They can do this verbally or silently. They can praise God through offering, testimony, prayer, and living a life of holiness. Praise and worship should never focus on the one praising and worshipping. The focus always should be on God!

I love it when true praise goes forth because it's powerful and it causes true believers to reflect personally on God's goodness in their lives. Praise expresses how valuable God is to us!

ASK YOURSELF

Why do I praise?

PONDER THIS

There is joy in your sacrifice of praise to God.

CHAPTER 24

DON'T RESURRECT TRADITIONS THAT DON'T BRING HIM GLORY

When I was growing up, I remember looking forward to jelly beans and chocolate bunnies at Easter. Although my parents and my church tried to teach me that Easter Sunday was about Jesus' resurrection and not my Easter basket, I couldn't quite grasp the importance. My little mind could not get past the thoughts of jellybeans and chocolate bunnies!

Paul wrote in 1 Corinthians that we should put away childish things when we grow up (See 1 Corinthians 13:11). This principle is so true when it comes to celebrating Resurrection Sunday (Easter). When a believer is filled with the Holy Spirit, the Spirit guides and reveals truth to him or her. Each year as you grow and mature in your faith, God, by His Spirit, will give you an even clearer revelation of the resurrection's meaning.

Jesus absolutely paid it all for us on the cross. He not only paid it all, but His resurrection gives us complete victory over sin and death—once and for all. His completed work includes not only shedding His blood for us, but also getting up from the grave for us. His resurrection means so much to us. The reason is that at the very core of it, there is a confident assurance that we too can live victoriously. We also have a steadfast hope no matter what we may face on this side of eternity.

I have put away my Easter basket. I have replaced it with a renewed sense of passion, energy, authentic worship for, and appreciation of Jesus. This joy that Jesus has given me lasts much longer than any chocolate bunny I've ever tasted!

Ask Yourself

What do I need to put away so I can celebrate Easter this year?

Ponder This

Easter is what being a Christian is all about. It symbolizes our death to sin and our resurrection to life in Him.

SO WHAT?

You go to church. You are religious—so what? You faithfully attend church every Sunday. You even put an offering in the basket when it's passed—so what? You carry a Bible under your arm and open it up every now and then—so what? You are a member of a church—so what? You no longer fall asleep during a sermon—so what?

"So what?" This is the question that many people who profess to be Christians need to ask themselves. Jesus declares in Matthew 7:22-23 that many are sitting around "doing" what appears to be God's work, but they are not in relationship with Him. He says, "Many will say to Me on that day, 'Lord, Lord, did we not prophesy in Your name, and in Your name cast out demons, and in Your name perform many miracles?' And then I will declare to them, 'I never knew you; *depart from me, you who practice lawlessness*'" (emphasis added).

Jesus is saying, "So what?" in this scripture. Until people truly profess Jesus Christ as Lord and believe it in their hearts to the point where they are changed and transformed into Christ's image, they are not saved. Instead, they are living in the realm of "so what?" This mindset promotes "doing" church instead of actively working to advance His kingdom. Ultimately, it will keep us from His kingdom if we are not living in His will.

ASK YOURSELF

What am I "doing" as a religious habit instead of being in relationship with God?

PONDER THIS

Being a Christian is more than just going to church on Sunday. It's doing God's will.

CHAPTER 26

EXTRA STRENGTH,
NEW AND IMPROVED

I've always wondered if products that make claims such as, "extra strength" or "new and improved," are factual or are they just marketing ploys to increase sales. In reality, what makes a product new and improved or a little bit stronger than the previous version?

Just as these marketers attempt to increase their sales, where do we stand as God's children when we make claims to be "new and improved" Christians? We don't necessarily say we are "new and improved" or that our Christianity now carries a greater potency. However, we do say things such as, "I am so glad the Lord has changed my heart," or "I'm glad I've got a new outlook on life," or "I've got a new way to walk and a new way to talk." These are claims we make all the time. Do they have any substance?

Marketers say their products are better. Perhaps they are or maybe they just look that way through new packaging. As Christians, are we really better after we've experienced God's grace, or like the new product packaging do we just appear to be better because we've learned to act better as Christians? Are we really improved or is it just a ploy?

The truth is a new and improved Believer not only has a new look but he or she is also consistent. Being a child of God is not a one-time deal. The Bible says we should become a new creature in Christ once we commit ourselves to Him (See 2 Cor. 5:17). "New and improved" for us means we are truly being transformed into Christ's image. With that transformation comes a new way of walking and talking that should be exemplified in every area and aspect of our lives.

ASK YOURSELF

Why do we work so hard to fool everyone when God really wants us to become who He has called us to be?

PONDER THIS

Too many of us in the body of Christ claim we are "new and improved." Yet, like laundry detergent or soft drinks, that claim is only a gimmick.

CHAPTER 27

DO WE REALLY WANT WHAT
GOD WANTS FOR US?

Lately I've been wondering if preaching and teaching the Bible in an honest and life transforming way is really worth it. Sounds ridiculous, right? The apostle Paul encouraged his mentee, Timothy, that there would come a day when people would not want to hear God's truth:

> For the time will come when they will not endure sound doctrine; but wanting to have their ears tickled, they will accumulate for themselves teachers in accordance to their own desires, and will turn away their ears from the truth and will turn aside to myths. But you, be sober in all things, endure hardship, do the work of an evangelist, fulfill your ministry.
> —2 Timothy 4:3-5

My friend recently said that it's amazing that any true Bible teaching church grows in today's culture. That is because only churches teaching unsound doctrine seem to be growing. I love to preach and teach God's Word, but there are times when I wonder if it makes any difference. I truly believe we are living in the last days. However, it is clear to me that some Christians do not want to hear the unadulterated Word of God. People hear the Word, but many are not living the Word. Why is that?

In the scripture, where Paul talked about people "wanting to have their ears tickled," he meant that people only want to hear what makes them feel good. They want to be affirmed in what they are doing. God gave His Word to us not only to encourage us to live righteously, but also to convict us about sin. The reality is that most sound biblical preaching will cut, not tickle.

So what are preachers and Christians who love God's Word to do? The answer is that we cannot let the crowd dictate the message we preach. Even if people do not want to hear it, we must preach it anyway!

ASK YOURSELF

Am I allowing God's Word to tickle me or cut me?

PONDER THIS

God wants to change and transform us, whether we want it or not!

CHAPTER 28

MOTHERS MAKE THE WORLD GO 'ROUND

In Matthew 15:21-29, we read about a mother who fights desperately for the spiritual health of her daughter. The text teaches us that the daughter has been afflicted with a demonic spirit. The mother, although a Gentile, approaches Jesus to ask him to heal her. Jesus initially denies her request, but she pursues Him all the more vigorously. The woman's faith moves Jesus so much that He heals her daughter.

What can we learn from this Gentile woman? We see that a mother's love is a love that fights. It's a love that believes. It's a love that will take on scorn, ridicule, and persecution for the benefit of her children. Mothers often give that final push that is needed to assist and encourage their children to go forth. A mother's love sounds and looks much like our Savior's love. It's selfless and it's sacrificial.

As Christians, we should admire the "never give up" spirit in our mothers. If the mother in Matthew had given up her pursuit of Jesus, her daughter's life would have been a tragedy. Mothers today do the same thing for their children. This love is reflects Christ's love for us. Thank God for godly mothers.

ASK YOURSELF

Who needs to know I will never give up on him or her?

PONDER THIS

A mother's love is symbolic of Jesus' unconditional love for us.

CHAPTER 29

PRACTICALITY VS. SPIRITUALITY

One of Satan's biggest traps for Christians is wrong perspective. As maturing Christians, we often struggle to understand and to see things from God's perspective. We have been shaped by our culture, ideology, education, experiences, and environment so much that our perspective is based on those things more than it is based on faith, God's Word, and the revelation the Holy Spirit gives.

That is why Romans 12:1-2 is such a foundational scripture for the follower of Jesus Christ. The apostle Paul wrote to the church at Rome:

> Therefore, I urge you, brethren, by the mercies of God, to present your bodies a living and holy sacrifice, acceptable to God, which is your spiritual service of worship. And do not be conformed to this world, but be transformed by the renewing of your mind, so that you may prove what the will of God is, that which is good and acceptable and perfect.
> —Rom. 12:1-2

This text teaches us that if we only see things from a natural perspective, we cannot know and do God's will. God, by His Holy Spirit, has to transform us by renewing our minds. We will not realize what God desires for us by doing what we normally do. The very definition of practical is "operating within the norms." Most Christians want to do what seems to be practical and not what is spiritual.

If we only operate in what we practice (our normal every-day activities), we never can understand God's will. We will function in what we know and not in His will. Believers must sacrifice themselves completely. This means we have to die to our selfish thoughts, our cultural norms, our self-ideologies, our intellects, and to ourselves. God wants us to function in His will, not in what seems practical to us because our thoughts are not His thoughts and our ways are not His ways (See Isa. 55:8).

Ask Yourself

Where in my life am I using practical thinking when I should be using spiritual thinking?

Ponder This

Spiritual thinking can only come from obedience to God and His Word.

MANY DON'T WANT THIS ROAD

Authentic Christianity is not popular in today's culture, but "entertainment Christianity" certainly is. Entertainment Christianity tells us what we want to hear. It's a Christianity that allows us to be comfortable in our sin. It's a Christianity that does not convict us or lead us to transformation.

Jesus said in John 6 that to be in a real relationship with Him, a person had to eat of His flesh and drink of His blood. Jesus was calling people to a full commitment. He wanted people to ingest Him symbolically so He would become a part of their total being.

After Jesus preached this, many decided not to follow Him any longer. Even today, many people, after counting the cost, do not want what Jesus offers us in authentic Christianity.

Where do you stand?

Ask Yourself

Am I participating in authentic Christianity or entertainment Christianity?

Ponder This

Those who fully commit to Christ will live forever.

CHAPTER 31

IS IT WORTH IT?

How many times have you asked yourself, "Is what I'm going through worth all the pain I am feeling?" Satan is good at what he does. One of his greatest tricks is orchestrating circumstances and people to get you to think that what you're going through is a permanent situation! Don't forget that storms always come to an end. That is why the apostle Paul encouraged us to forget those things that lie behind and to press on toward the goal of the prize of God's upward call in Christ Jesus (See Phil. 3:13-14). You are not a victim of your circumstances. You are a victor in Christ Jesus!

Stop holding on to yesterday's news. Did you have a disagreement with a loved one? Apologize and press on. Not getting along with your spouse? Decide today that you will do your part to get along. Is your boss trying to harm you? Pray for him or her and all those who spitefully use you.

Whatever hurt or harm you are experiencing today is not a permanent situation. It seems permanent because you've not given it to the One who can deal with it. God said in His Word that He would give us a peace that surpasses all understanding. I believe He will give us that perfect peace when we fully rely on Him. Let go and let God have His way in your life.

Be delivered and be set free!

ASK YOURSELF

What does God want me to do with the "right now" of my life?

PONDER THIS

God's Word says He knows the plan for our lives. That plan is not to harm us but to give us a great future and a great hope (See Jer. 29:11).

CHAPTER 32

DON'T THINK YOU CAN MAKE IT? THINK AGAIN!

Though you can't see what lies ahead of you right now, it doesn't mean that God's plan for your life is not going to happen. Beyond the storm, beyond the rain clouds, beyond the fog, and beyond your tears, is the kingdom dream God has for you. Though the vision tarries, wait on it. Don't you even think about quitting. You've come too far to turn back now! "For we walk by faith, not by sight" (2 Cor. 5:7).

At every turn of our lives, God's desire is to develop and grow our faith. My best moments have been my hardest moments. This revelation doesn't come to us until we persevere through the tough moments. Leading a ministry and leading God's people have been and still are a great challenge. I've experienced much heartache along the way. However, God is so awesome that if you will trust Him every heartache will be reversed, every trial will turn to a triumph, and every storm will eventually cease! This God we serve and worship is the God of great reversals.

I recently preached a message entitled "Getting Me Out of the Mix." God has said to us that He would not leave us nor forsake us. He also has said that no weapon formed against us shall prosper. So if our lives continue to stay on the wrong side of goodness, God is not the one who is missing the mark, we are. I want you to know that there is a better "you" inside of you. It is God's desire and plan to get the "you" that's inside of you to walk in victory.

> Therefore if anyone is in Christ, he is a new creature; the old things passed away; behold, new things have come.
> —2 Cor. 5:17

ASK YOURSELF

Who does God want me to believe and to trust when life gets difficult?

PONDER THIS

God loves you too much to let your life end in a miserable state. Trust Him!

CHAPTER 33

SUMMER BLUES

We often think of the winter season as the time of year when we feel down and depressed, but I have discovered that many Christians suffer from the blues in the summer months.

Why? The summer brings with it many things that distract us from God. The sun, beaches, vacations, backyard barbecues, and the other great activities that infiltrate our lives in the summer pull us away from worship and devotional time with our Savior.

God's Word says He who has begun a good work in us will complete it (See Phil. 1:6). However, there is a condition to this promise. We must delight ourselves in Him.

Unfortunately, during the summer season we end up delighting ourselves in everything other than God. So what is the end result? After the sun fades, the vacation ends, and the ribs are all gone, we find ourselves depressed. When we put all of our hope in things that aren't eternal, we set ourselves up for disappointment.

So what should you do? Enjoy your summer vacation, but don't forget your relationship with God.

ASK YOURSELF

How can I make God part of my family's summer fun?

PONDER THIS

God wants a relationship with us 24/7, not just on Sunday at 11 A.M.

CHAPTER 34

WHY SHOULD WE FAST AND PRAY?

The Christian life is one of commitment and sacrifice unto God. However, some of today's Christian leaders get this twisted. Instead of teaching that the Christian journey is about giving, they make people think it's about getting. They tell people that Christians have the power and authority to manipulate God into giving them what they want.

As Christians, we must always be cognizant of the fact that life does not center on our dreams and desires but on God's will. That is why the apostle Paul urged us in Romans 12:1 to present ourselves as a living sacrifice that is holy and acceptable to God. He also said we should do this (surrender and submission) so our lives prove to be living testimonies of His will.

Isaiah 58 addresses the issue of sincere prayer and fasting. The writer declares that authentic fasting and prayer is not about God hearing *us* but about *our* hearing God. He proclaims that deliverance and victory take place when God's people earnestly and sincerely seek Him through humility and submission.

Christ declared in Matthew 17:21 that there were some things in life that could only be dealt with by prayer and fasting. Fasting is a valuable tool that allows a Christian to seek God's face for clarity, direction, and victory over a physical, mental, emotional, or spiritual hurdle. At the foundation of any authentic fast, there must be a genuine desire for repentance and transformation. Without that, a fast is nothing more than a diet guised in the name of spirituality.

Are you in a season of struggle where you need God to do something extraordinary on your behalf? Fast, pray, and press into God like never before! Seek His face for direction and for your breakthrough. Be specific on what you need God to do for you. Most of all, expect and believe by faith that God will do it according to His will.

Ask Yourself

When I pray and fast, how can I focus more on giving and less on getting?

Ponder This

Renewing the mind through fasting and prayer brings clarity of God's perfect will.

CHAPTER 35

KNOWING GOD'S VOICE

The key to effective prayer is knowing how to discern God's voice from other voices. Many Christians struggle to determine whether or not God is speaking to them through His Holy Spirit. This is because they do not know God intimately enough to be confident that it's His voice they are hearing.

Prayer is a two-way communication process. It involves both speaking and listening. We must speak to God via prayer according to His Word. So the very things we pray for and about should line up with God's will, which is found in His Word, the Bible. Additionally, effective prayer involves listening to God's answers and directions. Many people don't do enough listening to and waiting for God's answers. Subsequently, they end up following their own desires.

Being a Christian does not automatically give a person the ability to know God's voice. There is effort involved. For example, a newborn baby learns his parents' voices through repetition. He hears the sound, tone, and style of his parents repeatedly because the parents continually talk to their new-born. Imagine if the parents never spoke to their newborn child! That newborn would not be able to recognize his parents' voices because he would not have had the opportunity to become familiar with them. Such is the case of the Christian. We must repeatedly hear God's voice, through His Word. In hearing His voice we can become so familiar with it and gain the necessary confidence.

We listen to God in our quiet devotional time and through studying His written and preached Word. When we learn to discipline ourselves in this way, we recognize God's voice, which is distinct and consistent. His voice and what He says never contradicts His Word or will for our lives. When we know God's voice and yield in obedience to His calling and direction, the results are a life of success and peace!

ASK YOURSELF

In what ways can I learn to know God's voice better?

PONDER THIS

The more we learn to be still and listen, the more we know God's voice.

CHAPTER 36

SALVATION IS NOT WHAT YOU THINK IT IS

I have pastored long enough now to realize there are many who sit in the pews on Sunday morning but really do not have a relationship with Christ. Flat out, they are not saved. To "be saved" means to have a restored, redeemed, and real relationship with God through believing in Jesus Christ, His Son. This belief leads to life transformation.

Many Christians have been exposed to religion but never to Christ. One can be in a religious setting all of his or her life and still never have a true encounter with Christ. Jesus declares this in Matthew 7:23 in which he says that many will come to Him at the Great White Throne of judgment and He will say, "I never knew you; *depart from me.*"

A true encounter with Christ encompasses three major components:

1. **Repentance:** a deep sense of sorrow accompanied by a desire to turn away from sin and toward God.
2. **Redemption:** a basic understanding that Jesus Christ has purchased us with His blood and we are made whole only through this action.
3. **Reformation:** A changed life (transformation). This is the lifelong process of sanctification. It's marked by becoming a disciple and being transformed into Christ's image and likeness in actions, thoughts, deeds, and works.

If you are stuck in "religion" but do not know Christ's saving grace, I pray you move into salvation and get beyond religion.

ASK YOURSELF

Am I saved?

PONDER THIS

It is possible to faithfully attend church and not have a saving relationship with Jesus Christ.

CHAPTER 37

IT'S NOT A DEAD END

With God, there are no dead ends, boundaries, or limitations. God's very nature is transcendent. This means He has no boundaries or limits. In life, it is easy to feel as if we've come to a dead end that leads to despair and hopelessness.

However, the apostle Paul reminds us that to live is Christ and to die is gain (See Phil. 1:21). At the time of the writing of this passage, Paul was dealing with his own personal dilemma. He struggled with staying here on earth to spread the gospel or dying and being in the Lord's eternal presence. Life itself, even when we get to the end, is not a dead end. Physical death is actually the beginning point for eternity. Praise the name of the Lord our God!

It is critical for Christians to know there are no dead ends with God. Often, it is at the dead end that God does His best work. It's that place where we surrender our own efforts and futile attempts at making "it" happen and fully surrender to God. The dead end is where we say, "Where do I go now?" In desperation and anguish we then fall to our knees and cry out, "Father, I stretch my hand to thee. There is no other help I know."

God's response to our dead end anguish is, "Good, I see you've exhausted all other devices and avenues for your situation. Now I can work with you and through you." God takes our dead ends and makes them part like the Red Sea. He takes our dead ends and heals diseases. He takes our dead ends and provides rams in the bush. He takes our dead ends and sends His Son to the cross so we can live.

Wow, your dead end is not what you thought it was, is it?

ASK YOURSELF

Do I have a dead end I need to turn over to the Lord?

PONDER THIS

For Christians, death is gain.

CHAPTER 38

ENJOY THE JOURNEY
AS GOD PROCESSES YOU

A good friend of mine blessed my soul with a powerful word of encouragement! As our church began to grow and transition from a small family church to a very powerful and impacting kingdom church, there was resistance along the way. He advised me to enjoy the journey and not to worry about the resistance. To focus on the resistance would be to take my eyes off what God was doing, he said. What a word of encouragement!

New wine needs new wineskins. When God develops you, He is placing you in the season of "new wine." We can't stay as we were. If you are trying to "maintain," you are holding yourself back from what God is trying to do in you. You're not going to enjoy the journey if you're not willing to go where God says you must go!

Are you resistant to the changes and adjustments God is causing in you? If you're OK with the place you currently are, then you are blocking your progress. Discipleship has no stagnation. A true disciple embraces the need to grow spiritually! If you aren't attempting to grow by being discipled, then you are holding your team back. If you can't be coached, taught, disciplined, trained, or held accountable, then you're holding yourself back.

At the same time, as you decide to follow Christ in a greater way, remember to enjoy the journey. You are in the midst of God doing something awesome!

It is my prayer that you join God at His work in your life. I also encourage you not to resist the flow by grumbling, complaining, and looking for yesterday to be today. Yesterday is gone, so let's rejoice, celebrate, and thank God for it. Today is here. God's counsel is not to take this moment for granted. Tomorrow is coming, so now is the time to prepare for that tomorrow. Jesus promised He would build His church and the gates of hell would not prevail against it. He is building His church by building you.

Enjoy the journey. I plan to!

ASK YOURSELF

Have I been resisting what God is trying to do in me?

PONDER THIS

God will get the glory through your life, so ease up and let Him have His way!

CHAPTER 39

CAN YOU HANDLE
THE PROMOTION?

Most Christians don't understand that promotion comes from God. Only God truly elevates His children. Manipulation, strong-arming, brown-nosing, scheming, and conniving are all tactics that people use who have not learned to trust God fully. What's amazing is that these tactics may get a person to a temporary spot, but in the end, they will not last nor will they be blessed. The wealth of the wicked is stored up for the righteous (See Prov. 13:22).

Some people have not been promoted because God knows they cannot handle it. God's Word says that he who is faithful over a few things will be given much more (See Matt. 25:21). Most of us want God to elevate us. However, after examination, the evidence reveals that some people have not been faithful over what they have. Instead, they are filled with concealed sin, apathy, laziness, and a heart not knitted toward God.

God is wise. There is nothing foolish about Him. He must ask, "Why would I promote anyone who has not demonstrated he can handle his current position?" If a person can't get to work on time, why would God allow him or her to become a supervisor? If a servant can't give an honorable offering to God from his or her income, why would God make that person a leader in the church? If a servant can't get excited about a small ministry, why would God bless him or her with a bigger ministry to oversee? If a servant can't stop cheating on his or her taxes, fornicating, lusting, and doing things that are not pleasing to God, why would God bless that person with material blessings? As the Bible says, "Do not be deceived, God is not mocked; for whatever a man sows, this he will also reap" (Gal. 6:7).

ASK YOURSELF

In what ways am I worthy of God's promotion?

PONDER THIS

Actions speak louder than words. If you are living outside of God's will, don't expect God to bless your life.

CHAPTER 40

ARE YOU HIGH?

It's great to feel spiritually "high," but it's not good to want to remain high. Too often in Christianity, we want our relationship with Christ to be validated by a feeling. The problem with that is our feelings are like the stock market—up today and down tomorrow. It is true that when we are walking in the center of God's will, we can feel His joy and power. Psalm 16:11 confirms that in His presence there is "fullness of joy."

However, the joy of the Lord is not a feeling, nor is it just an emotional high. The joy that only the Lord can bring is a permanent sense of His fullness, power, and presence. This joy contains a depth and a fortress that trials, enemies, disappointments, and setbacks cannot penetrate. When we confuse happiness and emotional highs with the joy of the Lord, we don't know how to walk in this joy the Lord has offered us.

How do you experience the everlasting joy of the Lord? It's almost too simple to believe. The answer is found right in God's Word. Jesus commands us to abide in Him and to make a decision to allow Him to abide in us. He says if we do this, we will bear much fruit (See John 15:7-8).

I've come to discover that getting high off a great sermon, worship experience, or conference just isn't good enough. The emotional highs we get from those things are temporal and unsustainable. They can turn us into spiritual junkies, running to every revival, church conference, and gospel concert we can find. No, what we ought to desire is what David declared in the Psalms, that we may "dwell in the house of the LORD" forever (See Ps. 27:4).

ASK YOURSELF

What can I do to avoid "getting high" in the Lord?

PONDER THIS

Don't get high! Instead, abide in Him and walk in everlasting joy (See Gal. 6:7).

CHAPTER 41

COVERED IN IT

Sin is an ugly three-letter word. With God, there are no degrees of sin. He hates all sin.

We all know what the major sins are. Then there are the subtle sins—the ones that are more difficult to notice. They are the ones we can justify as "small," such as cheating a little on our taxes, taking supplies from our office, flirting a little on the job, and giving God less than our best time, talent, and treasure. These subtle sins can soon turn into larger ones, such as sleeping with someone to whom we are not married, getting deep into debt, and even skipping church.

Sometimes people walk in sin for so long that they don't recognize it for what it is. The Bible warns us about this in Romans 12:2: "Do not be conformed to this world." People justify sinful behaviors by saying, "Everyone else is doing it so it must not be so bad." However, Christians must always remember that we are not called to be like everyone else. If being like everyone else becomes the standard by which we live, then we cannot call ourselves followers of Jesus.

King David's story in 2 Samuel chapters 11-12, is a classic example of how sin can cover you. David sinned by committing adultery with Bathsheba. Then he sinned by plotting to have her husband, Uriah, killed in battle. He committed adultery and murder! Because he was the king and was extremely popular, no one held him accountable. He was so covered in the cloak of sin that he did not even recognize how deep he was into it. God had to send Nathan the prophet to show David his sin.

When people entangle themselves in secret sin and do not allow anyone to hold them accountable, it is easy for them to get comfortable in that sin. When we wear a piece of clothing for a long time, it becomes ugly. However, we are so used to it that we don't see it for what it is.

Are you covered in the cloak of sin? Take it off, repent, and ask for forgiveness.

ASK YOURSELF

For which "small" sins do I need to ask forgiveness?

PONDER THIS

There are no degrees of sin with God—just as murder is sin, so are lust and greed.

CHAPTER 42

DON'T BE A CONSUMER

It's unfortunate, but our culture of consumerism has infiltrated the church. Members and prospective members of the body of Christ now look at the church with a consumer's mentality.

One definition of "consumer" is someone who pursues and uses goods for his own gain. Another is someone who preys on an organism for its resources. As consumers, people in the body think the church is a grocery store in which they can go up and down the aisles picking and choosing those goods or services that are beneficial to them.

The Word teaches that "we" as individuals are the church. We are the members that make up the body. Our role is not to consume but to serve and give. Romans says it this way,

> Let love be without hypocrisy Abhor what is evil; cling to what is good. Be devoted to one another in brotherly love; give preference to one another in honor; not lagging behind in diligence, fervent in spirit, serving the Lord; rejoicing in hope, persevering in tribulation, devoted to prayer, contributing to the needs of the saints, practicing hospitality.
> —Rom.12:9-13

Notice the theme of this scripture is one of contribution, not taking.

What's wrong with the consumerism mentality? People who think this way do not understand that they, not the pastor, facility, or ministry, are the church. Jesus commands those of "us" in the church to serve one another, not to consume from one another. Additionally, consumers have a tendency to change stores once they tire of a certain product or can get it for a better price elsewhere. Consumerism does not promote loyalty to God or service to others. It promotes selfishness. Consumerism leads people to seek what *they* want, not what God wants for them. It does not promote the Matthew 6:33 idea of "seek first His kingdom and His righteousness" but instead destroys it.

Don't be a consumer or you may find yourself completely out of God's will!

Ask Yourself

How do I treat my church as a consumer and how can I change that?

Ponder This

It might have walls of steel, but the church is only as strong as its members.

CHAPTER 43

ACTIVATE THE ACCOUNT

Have you ever wondered why so many Christians don't seem to act like Christians at all? The truth is there are many people who think they are Christians but they have not trusted in Jesus as their Savior and Redeemer through faith and repentance.

There are many Christians who simply have not activated their salvation accounts. Ephesians 1:13 teaches us that the Holy Spirit is given to the believer at the moment of salvation: "In Him, you also, after listening to the message of truth, the gospel of your salvation—having also believed, you were sealed in Him with the Holy Spirit of promise."

Ephesians 5 says that we must take an active role in allowing the Holy Spirit to work and transform our lives that we might live as Christians. Ephesians 5:18-19 gives us this command: "Do not get drunk with wine, for that is dissipation, but be filled with the Spirit, speaking to one another in psalms and hymns and spiritual songs, singing and making melody with your heart to the Lord."

When you get a new credit card there is normally a sticker on it with a toll-free number that says, "To activate this card, call this number." This is similar to what Paul is commanding us to do in Ephesians 5. When believers do not make an active decision to die to self and continuously crucify sinful desires, they never allow the Holy Spirit to become fully active and enabled in their lives.

Thus, we find many who profess to be Christians, but their actions and conduct are far away from God's character and Word. It is only in the Holy Spirit and the process of regeneration that the true child of God can live a life reflective of Christ.

71

ASK YOURSELF

Have you activated your salvation account?

PONDER THIS

The Holy Spirit is like a free "gift with purchase" when you receive Christ and become regenerated in Him.

CHAPTER 44

WHO LIKES ACCOUNTABILITY?

The principle of accountability is woven throughout Scripture. To become a disciple of Jesus Christ is by its very nature a process of constant accountability. No Christian was born to live on an island! All Christians who live as disciples will have an intentional setup of accountability, because without it, growth will not happen.

Ephesians 4:11-12 tells us why God gives pastors and teachers to the church: He knows that without ordained and gifted leadership, His sheep will go astray. It reads, "And He gave some as apostles, and some as prophets, and some as evangelists, and some as pastors and teachers, for the equipping of the saints for the work of service, to the building up of the body of Christ."

God intentionally set up the process of accountability that is to be handled by the pastor. Accountability simply boils down to training, equipping, and disciplining a person to serve God through ministry (the local church).

Accountability and/or being held accountable are principles that contradict the world's ideology. The secular worldview says, "Be your own boss, do your own thing, and answer to no one. No one but you can or should tell you what to do." Even though this is the cultural norm, it is absolutely not a biblical one. Proverbs 14:12 teaches us why this mentality is dangerous: "There is a way which seems right to a man, but its end is the way of death."

Although we don't like being held accountable, Scripture affirms it is an absolute necessity.

Ask Yourself

Who is helping you live for Jesus 100 percent?

Ponder This

Accountability is meant to work as iron sharpens iron, so you can serve Him to your fullest.

CHAPTER 45

LORD, REVIVE US AGAIN

When I was growing up in the church, "revival" meant a week of preaching by some evangelist or preacher. I always thought it was just an opportunity for a preacher to get God's people fired up through good preaching.

However, God's revival for His people is much more than just a weeklong series of worship services. To revive something means to bring it back to consciousness and to restore it from a depressive or inactive state. Using God's definition, "revived" is the state in which He desires all His children to stay.

There is never a moment when Christians should be inactive or unconscious in their walk with Christ. The truth is, most of us are not feeling revived because we are too bogged down with the cares of this world—our jobs, our activities, and our own agendas.

May I suggest that revival begins in the individual Christian? Revival starts when you decide to knit your heart toward God and His agenda!

ASK YOURSELF

What steps do I need to take to get "revived"?

PONDER THIS

When you choose to seek Him and His Kingdom first, you will be revived!

CHAPTER 46

SILENT ABOUT THE THINGS
THAT MATTER

Dr. Martin Luther King Jr. once said, "Our lives begin to end the day we become silent about things that matter." What a profound and powerful statement! While Dr. King said this in the context of segregation and racial injustice, his words and the principle within them ring true about today's church.

What do people who go to church really care about? Does the current body of Christ care about what Christ cares about? If so, how is that reflected in our everyday living? (Before you answer this question, be mindful that *we* are the body of Christ!)

Today's church is not mindful of God's agenda. Our behavior reflects what is really important to us. As a whole, our daily living and our daily concerns are not showing others that we have the mind of Christ. We wear our Christianity like costume jewelry. It's only good for certain outfits and certain occasions!

We "do" great church, but some of us are silent in our witness for Christ. We love to shout and dance but we are silent when we see other Christians compromising. We nod and say, "Amen" when the preacher preaches, but we are silent when the message convicts us. We are energized and committed when it comes to the things we want, but we are silent when it comes to what God wants for us. We go into debt for material possessions but we are silent when it comes to supporting God's kingdom agenda with our finances. We join churches but we are silent in being committed. We work our tails off in the workplace but we are silent when work is needed at the church. We are quick to criticize spiritual leadership but we are silent about our own apathy.

When God looks at His children's hearts, I think He is most concerned with the kind of fruit we are bearing. As we envision Christ's agony and pain on the cross, His sacrifice should scream loudly in our hearts and minds. Have we turned a deaf ear to our Savior's convicting and redemptive work? The volume has been turned all the way down! Did Jesus bear the cross for our convenience?

Ask Yourself

How much longer will I remain silent?

Ponder This

When we are silent about things that matter, we are not living in Christ's fullness.

CHAPTER 47

WHEN GOD BUILDS A CHURCH

I read a book several years ago by Bob Russell, senior pastor of the 15,000-member Southeast Christian Church in Louisville, Kentucky. He wrote about ten principles that concern God in building His church.

One of the principles he outlines is the principle of excellence. Any healthy God-honoring church must have excellence at the core of its character and personality. Excellence starts with a desire to be pleasing to God. It continues with an understanding of God's will and His character. When we love God the way He wants us to love Him, an excellent spirit follows suit.

Excellence causes God's children to be passionate in their thinking and ministry. Apathy, slothfulness, and lethargy cannot reside in the Christian who desires to be in an authentic relationship with Jesus Christ. Excellence demonstrates a heart knitted toward God.

When God builds a church, He first builds character. Without godly character and godly integrity, the number of people in a church will not matter. God is building you one step at a time. He is working on your character. Don't be surprised when trials come (See 1 Peter 4:12). He is building your character!

Ask Yourself

Where do I need to increase my commitment to excellence?

Ponder This

A healthy church begins with people who pursue excellence.

CHAPTER 48

WHY STRUGGLES KEEP SLAPPING US IN THE FACE

Doesn't it make you angry that life keeps making you do retakes? I don't know about you, but I find myself consistently asking God why I have to learn certain lessons over and over again. I am convinced God does have a sense of humor. However, even while He is being humorous, He is molding and shaping us into His Son's image.

In recent days, God has revealed that most of my struggles are self-induced. In this Christian journey, we are going to face trials and suffering for the cause of Christ. However, we bring a lot of this on ourselves. The truth is that it is not the struggle which gets us down. It is how we respond to the challenges that lead us down the path of pity and depression.

We refuse to keep the main thing the main thing. We compare ourselves to others. We get upset because we don't have what the Jones' have. We buy into the "Extreme Makeover" mentality. We convince ourselves we are not good enough, even though our Creator tells us we have are fearfully and wonderfully made. We're caught up in what we don't have, but fail to rejoice in the Lord for what we do have.

I am convinced that struggles would stop slapping us in the face if we would do as the apostle Paul commands in Philippians 4:6: "Be anxious for nothing, but in everything by prayer and supplication with thanksgiving let your requests be made known to God."

If you're anything like me, when struggles come, your first reaction isn't to pray. Because you don't make your requests and supplications known to God, anxiety gets tattooed across your forehead. The problem is this: It's not the struggles that hurt you. What hurts you is not going to the Master of your struggles and letting Him do what only He can do.

Ask Yourself

What kinds of struggles do I have that I need to give to the Lord?

Ponder This

Stop struggling and wrestling with life's trials. Put them in the Master's hands!

CHAPTER 49

A TRULY TRANSFORMED LIFE

Most Christians cannot figure out how it is possible to keep all of God's commandments, to live a holy life, and to glorify God in all they say and do. If pressed, they would tell you that the aforementioned goals are not even realistic. My response for those who make this statement is, "Why would God command us to do something that isn't possible?"

Sin is a nasty little word that prevents us from being transformed. For most of us, sin is one of those things we have to continually battle. Danny Lovett, author of the book, *Jesus Is Awesome*, wrote, "The biggest struggle with sin is in our thought life. The past comes up, worry presses in, discouragement passes by, evil thoughts about others drop in, and the devil suggests things unheard of."

It's this doggone sin thing that keeps us from fully glorifying God, obeying His commands, and living a holy life. This same disease called "sin" prevents us from being truly transformed into Christ's image. So how do we deal with this awful disease? Simple, by God's Word. We must know, study, meditate on, and memorize God's Word to truly combat sin and be transformed into Christ's image.

Here is a short story about how God's Word can transform a person. A pastor wanted to conquer sin in his life so he made three columns in the back of his Bible. In each column, he listed ten scriptures. Ten verses dealt with the lust of the eyes, ten verses dealt with the lust of the flesh, and the other ten dealt with the pride of life. He memorized all thirty verses. Whenever he was tempted, he would quote a scripture from that column of sin and pray for victory. If the temptation did not go away, he would quote another scripture and pray for victory. He would continue to quote scriptures and pray until God gave Him the victory.

God's Word can transform your life, but you must know that it can in order to become all He has ordained for you. As it says in the Bible, without His Word deep within your heart, you are like a ship that sets sail but is destined to reach the wrong island. "Let no one say when he is tempted, 'I am being tempted by God'; for God cannot be tempted by evil, and He Himself does not tempt anyone. But each one is tempted when he is carried away and enticed by his own lust. Then when lust has conceived, it gives birth to sin; and when sin is accomplished, it brings forth death" (James 1:13-16).

Ask Yourself

How can I better use God's Word to become what He has ordained for my life?

Ponder This

God will always give the victory.

CHAPTER 50

GIVING TO GET

The Christmas season normally is marked by chaos. Running to and from the malls, worrying over increased debt, and dealing with the pressure to find the right gifts, are only a some of the reasons why so many people end up stressed during this time of year.

What a shame it is that even some in the body of Christ get caught up in this mess and lose focus on the true reason for this season—the celebration of the birth of our Savior, Jesus Christ. The cookies, the gifts, the tree, and so on are supposed to be because God sent His Son.

Yet Jesus truly demonstrated to us that the Christmas season should be about giving, not receiving. He came to earth in the flesh only to die for our gain. He gave Himself as a ransom for many—for the gain of others, not Himself.

You can show people the real meaning of Christmas by focusing on Christ's birth instead of getting caught up in holiday details. Rather than spend your time and money on presents and decorating, why not give through tithing your time and money to the kingdom? Making Christ the center of your Christmas will cause others to stop and realize the stress isn't what it's all about—it's the gift of a baby, who became a man and died for our sins.

ASK YOURSELF

How will I celebrate my Savior's birth this year?

PONDER THIS

There is no greater gift than that of Jesus Christ, our Savior.

CHAPTER 51

LET'S DO WHAT WE DO, BUT LET'S DO IT BETTER

I recently read Tony Dungy's new book, *Quiet Strength*. He is the recently retired coach of the Super Bowl Champions, the Indianapolis Colts. He is also a remarkable leader and true Christian who stands for his faith regardless of his situation or circumstances. In reading the book, I was encouraged and excited that Tony is a humble leader who does not lead by intimidation or force. He leads with a quiet strength and a refreshing dose of personal integrity and humility rarely seen in our world today. Tony proves that genuine and effective leadership can and should look like Christ.

One of the things that encouraged me most was Tony's philosophy on team building. In building championship teams, he focused on personal integrity, character, accountability, teamwork, and consistency. The way Tony built his teams at both Tampa Bay and Indianapolis was to focus on what they believed in and never to waver from the path of their beliefs. In the midst of adversity and challenge, his teams never lost focus of what they believed. They did not make wholesale changes with personnel or with their philosophy. They stuck to it. In the fight to become champions, they always would say, "Let's do what we do and let's continue to get better at what we do."

This statement reminds me of the church. What we do in terms of developing disciples, holding each other accountable, living out God's Word, and challenging each other to share our faith and live as ambassadors for Christ, is exactly what we should be doing.

So let's continue to do what we do but let's get better at it. Let's take it up a notch and be champions for Jesus! Not one of us "arrived" spiritually last year. None of us can rest on last year's triumphs.

I urge you to join God in His work at your church. You don't have to worry about what the church down the street is doing. You just need to execute the plan and vision God has given your fellowship. Do what you do and continue to get better at it!

Ask Yourself

What does my church do and how can we get better at what we do?

Ponder This

The vision God gave you and your church is tailor-made for you. Just execute that vision and everything else will fall into place.

CHAPTER 52

BRING GOD TO YOUR BATTLE

The Lord has reminded us that we are in spiritual warfare so we must be on guard at all times and put on the full armor God (See Eph. 6:10-17).

Many times, we are in the spiritual war but we leave God out of the battle. Ephesians 6:10 advises us to be strong in God's might, not our own might. How do you know if you've left God out of the battle? Find out by reading the following principles:

1. You rarely pray. Your prayer life is so inconsistent that you don't regularly hear from God or get direction from God.
2. You rarely experience the joy of the Lord. Psalm 16:11 tells us that in God's presence there is fullness of joy. When God through relationship is not in our presence, we don't experience joy.
3. You constantly have doubt and feel overwhelmed. Feeling doubtful and overwhelmed are indicators that you're looking at your own devices to handle your battles. Walking with God and letting Him lead creates confidence in you.
4. You don't believe you can overcome the obstacle. Jesus calls us "overcomers" yet we miss this fact when we leave God out of the equation.

ASK YOURSELF

Have I been fighting my spiritual battles in my own strength?

PONDER THIS

God has equipped us for the battle. We just need to use the resources He has given us.

PW

LaVergne, TN USA
25 November 2009
165221LV00002B/1/P